NATURAL MARVELS

Breathtaking Chasms

WORLD
BOOK

World Book, Inc.
180 North LaSalle Street, Suite 900
Chicago, Illinois 60601
USA

For information about other World Book publications, please visit our website at www.worldbook.com or call 1-800-WORLDBK (967-5325).

For information about sales to schools and libraries, please call 1-800-975-3250 (United States) or 1-800-837-5365 (Canada).

Library of Congress Cataloging-in-Publication Data

Title: Breathtaking chasms.
Description: Chicago: World Book, Inc., a Scott Fetzer company, [2017] | Series: Natural marvels | Includes index.
Identifiers: LCCN 2016039085 | ISBN 9780716633648
Subjects: LCSH: Basins (Geology)--Juvenile literature. | Landforms--Juvenile literature. | Plate tectonics--Juvenile literature. | Grand Canyon (Ariz.)--Juvenile literature. | Mariana Trench--Juvenile literature. | Great Rift Valley--Juvenile literature.
Classification: LCC QE615 .B74 2017 | DDC 551.44--dc23
LC record available at https://lccn.loc.gov/2016039085

Over eons, the forces of nature have sculpted Earth in certain locations to create majestic landscapes of great beauty. Some of the most spectacular landforms are featured in this series of books. This image shows the Grand Canyon at sunrise.

This edition:
ISBN: 978-0-7166-3364-8 (hc.)
ISBN: 978-0-7166-3363-1 (set, hc.)

Also available as:
ISBN: 978-0-7166-3373-0
(e-book, EPUB3)

Printed in China by Shenzhen Wing King Tong Paper Products Co., Ltd., Shenzhen, Guangdong
1st printing March 2017

STAFF

Writer: Christine Sullivan

Executive Committee

President
Jim O'Rourke

Vice President and Editor in Chief
Paul A. Kobasa

Vice President, Finance
Donald D. Keller

Vice President, Marketing
Jean Lin

Vice President, International Sales
Maksim Rutenberg

Director, Human Resources
Bev Ecker

Editorial

Director, Digital and Print Content Development
Emily Kline

Editor, Digital and Print Content Development
Kendra Muntz

Manager, Science
Jeff De La Rosa

Editors, Science
William D. Adams
Nicholas V. Kilzer

Administrative Assistant, Digital and Print Content Development
Ethel Matthews

Manager, Contracts & Compliance (Rights & Permissions)
Loranne K. Shields

Manager, Indexing Services
David Pofelski

Graphics and Design

Senior Art Director
Tom Evans

Senior Designer
Don Di Sante

Media Editor
Rosalia Bledsoe

Senior Cartographer
John M. Rejba

Manufacturing/Production

Production/Technology Manager
Anne Fritzinger

Proofreader
Nathalie Strassheim

Table of Contents

Glossary There is a glossary of terms on page 38. Terms defined in the glossary are in type **that looks like this** on their first appearance on any spread (two facing pages). Words that are difficult to say are followed by a pronunciation (*pruh NUHN see AY shuhn*) the first time they are used.

Introduction

The three *landforms* (natural features on Earth's surface) covered in this book may look somewhat the same. They are all large *chasms* (*KAZ uhmz*) — deep openings or cracks in Earth's surface. But they were formed in very different ways.

One type of chasm is a *canyon*, a deep valley with steep sides. Arizona's Grand Canyon, in the southwestern United States, is unusually deep and has very steep sides. The Grand Canyon was formed by **erosion** (*ih ROH zhuhn*)— that is, by the wearing away of layers of rock and soil over time. The Colorado River has been wearing away and carving out the Grand Canyon for millions of years (see pages 8-17).

The Mariana Trench is a deep chasm at the bottom of the sea, in the western Pacific Ocean. One part of the trench, the Challenger **Deep,** is the deepest place on Earth. The Mariana Trench may look like the Grand Canyon, but it was not formed in the same way. **Plate tectonics** (*tehk TON ihks*) formed the Mariana Trench (see pages 28-29).

The third landform, the Great Rift Valley, is actually a long line of valleys cutting through much of the eastern part of the continent of Africa and an area in the southwestern part of the continent of Asia. This rift valley was also formed by plate tectonics, but it was formed in a different way from the Mariana Trench.

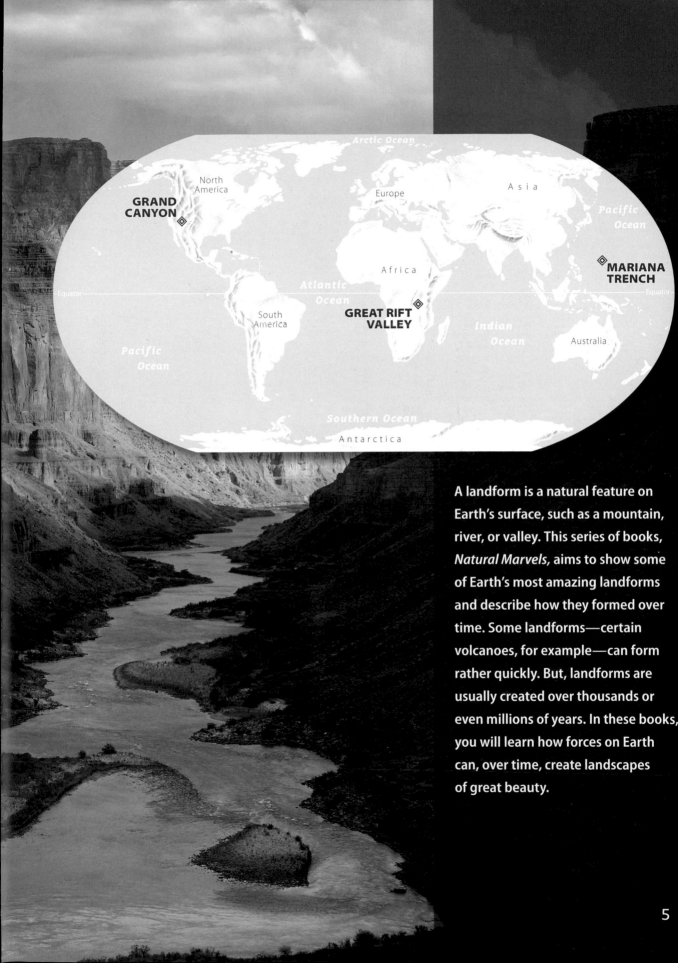

GRAND
CANYON ◇

MARIANA ◇
TRENCH

GREAT RIFT
VALLEY ◇

North
America

South
America

Atlantic
Ocean

Pacific
Ocean

Arctic Ocean

Europe

Africa

Asia

Pacific
Ocean

Indian
Ocean

Australia

Southern Ocean

Antarctica

Equator

Equator

A landform is a natural feature on Earth's surface, such as a mountain, river, or valley. This series of books, *Natural Marvels*, aims to show some of Earth's most amazing landforms and describe how they formed over time. Some landforms—certain volcanoes, for example—can form rather quickly. But, landforms are usually created over thousands or even millions of years. In these books, you will learn how forces on Earth can, over time, create landscapes of great beauty.

The Grand Canyon

Where Is the Grand Canyon and What's Special About It?

The Grand Canyon is in the southwestern United States, in the state of Arizona. The Colorado River runs through the canyon—one of the most amazing chasms in the world. The Grand Canyon is 1 mile (1.6 kilometers) deep. It ranges from less than 1 mile to 18 miles (1.6 to 29 kilometers) wide. It is about 277 miles (446 kilometers) long.

The layers of the Colorado **Plateau** (*pla TOH*), where the Grand Canyon is found, are made up of different types of rock, such as limestone (a type of rock made up mostly of calcite, a mineral form of calcium carbonate) and sandstone (formed when sand is cemented together by minerals or **pressure** as new layers form on top of existing layers). The rock layers in the Grand Canyon vary in shade and color, and the tones seem to change during the day as the direction of the sun's light changes. At sunset, the red and brown layers in the walls of the canyon are especially brilliant.

It is not just its size or beauty, however, that makes the Grand Canyon such a marvel. There are other canyons that are longer, deeper, wider, or more colorful. What is so impressive about the Grand Canyon is that the sides of its cliffs show the layers of rock that, over millions of years, built up the Colorado Plateau where the canyon is located. When we look at these layers, we are really looking back in time. Time over a huge span of years. **Geologic** time.

In the layers of rock, we can see the span of geologic time in the Grand Canyon.

UTAH

Lake Powell

Hildale
Colorado City
Kanab

Virgin River

Vermilion Cliffs

Fredonia

Colorado River
Paria R.

Paria Plateau

Marble Canyon

Virgin Mountains

Hurricane Cliffs

Uinkaret Plateau

Antelope Valley

Vermilion Cliffs

Jacob Lake

Echo Cliffs

Colorado Plateau

House Rock Valley

Kanab Creek

Kaibito Plateau

Grand Wash

Kanab Plateau

Kanab Canyon

Granite Narrows

Kaibab Plateau

North Canyon Wash

Marble Canyon

Lake Mead

Grand Wash Cliffs

GRAND CANYON NATIONAL PARK

Toroweap Valley
TOROWEAP POINT
VULCANS THRONE
LAVA FALLS RAPIDS

G R A N D   C A N Y O N

Supai

Havasu Creek

Middle Granite Gorge

GRAND CANYON NATIONAL PARK

POINT IMPERIAL

Colorado R.

Painted

RAMPART (SLOTH) CAVE

Shivwits Plateau

Sanup Plateau

POINT SUBLIME
Granite Gorge
Aztec Amphitheater

BRIGHT ANGEL POINT
North Rim
PHANTOM RANCH
CAPE ROYAL
MOHAVE POINT

Desert

GRAND CANYON NATIONAL PARK

Lower Granite Gorge

ARIZONA

Aubrey Cliffs

Coconino Plateau

HERMIT'S REST
Grand Canyon Village
MATHER POINT
South Rim
DESERT VIEW

Tusayan

Little Colorado R.

Cataract Cr.

Grand Wash Cliffs

Colorado River

Seperation Canyon

NATURAL BRIDGE
Lower Granite Gorge

| National park boundary | | City |
| Río | | Point of interest |

National park boundary ——————   City •
River ∿∿∿   Point of interest ◆

0   15   30 Miles
0   15   30   45 Kilometers

9

The Animals and Plants of the Grand Canyon

The area surrounding the Grand Canyon is mostly dry. Things that live in the canyon tend to be **adapted** to dry conditions. That means that these living things have changed over long periods of time to be able to survive in a place with little rain.

Hundreds of *species* (kinds) of birds live in the area of the Grand Canyon. It also has many other kinds of animals, including beavers, bighorn sheep, cougars (also called mountain lions), coyotes, elk, lizards, mule deer, and snakes. White-tailed Kaibab squirrels and pink Grand Canyon rattlesnakes live *only* in the area of the Grand Canyon.

Ponderosa pine, juniper, and piñon pine trees grow on the canyon's rim and at lower levels towards the southern end of the canyon. Aspen, fir, and spruce live at the higher areas in the northern end of the canyon. Cactuses grow throughout the canyon area, especially in low areas.

A California condor (top) looks over the Grand Canyon; yucca plants (above) grow in dry areas around the canyon, and deer drink from the Colorado River (left).

Above, a yellow-backed spiny lizard suns itself on a branch in the Grand Canyon; a lone pine tree (right) stands at the canyon's rim; a bighorn sheep (below) is surefooted and does not fear the steep cliffs of the Grand Canyon.

About the Grand Canyon

The California condor almost became extinct at the end of the last century. The Grand Canyon was repopulated with condors raised in captivity.

Light-colored layers of the Kaibab limestone and the Coconino sandstone make up the top portion and rim of the Grand Canyon.

Thick layers of siltstone, mudstone, and fine-grained sandstone make up the middle layers of the canyon. Rich in iron, these layers are reddish in color.

Layers of greenish and gray shale make up the lower layers of the canyon. They formed more than 500 million years ago.

The dark layers of rock at the bottom of the canyon formed almost 2 billion years ago. The Colorado River continues to wear away at this layer today.

Coyotes are common residents in and around Grand Canyon National Park.

The rare white-tailed Kaibab squirrel (above) is found only in Grand Canyon National Park.

Grand Canyon National Park has one of the richest ecosystems in the United States. It contains desert and forest and hundreds of species of birds, amphibians, mammals, and reptiles.

The Grand Canyon rattlesnake is pinkish in color and blends into the rocky terrain and cliff walls. It will usually avoid humans, and it rattles to warn people that they are getting too close.

The cougar (also called mountain lion or puma) normally avoids people, so it is rarely seen at the canyon.

Barrel cactus, Margarita fleabane, and Beavertail cactus are some of the desert plants that you may see at Grand Canyon National Park.

How Was the Grand Canyon Formed?

The Grand Canyon runs through the Colorado **Plateau.** The plateau's earliest and deepest rocks are about 2 billion years old. The Grand Canyon reveals all of the rock layers that have built up since to make the plateau.

The Grand Canyon is a good example of the power of **erosion** on Earth's surface. Erosion, the wearing away of rock and soil, is caused by such things as wind, moving water, and weather. For millions of years, the Colorado River (or scientists think possibly another, earlier river) has worked its way down through layer after layer of rock. Day by day, the river wore away tiny bits of the Colorado Plateau. Over time, the river made its own **channel** deeper and wider. In addition, sand, pebbles, and boulders carried by the river created a constant grinding and wearing action on the surrounding rocks.

It may surprise you to learn that, over time, water can wear away rock. If you turned on the garden hose in your back yard, you might not expect the water to make a huge hole in the ground. But perhaps you are not thinking about the effect flowing water can have over a long period of time. If you allowed the hose to run in your back yard for, say, 10,000 years, might it then create a giant hole? It likely would. That is how most **geologic** forces work. Slowly, over very long periods of time, moving water, wind, and other forces create the landscapes we see today.

Water running down a rock face in the canyon (left) has, over time, eroded the stone. Layers of harder rock were exposed as softer rock was eroded away, leaving a series of deep horizontal grooves. The forces of erosion acting on rocks can sometimes create unusual rock formations, such as the one seen below.

15

How Was the Grand Canyon Formed? *continued from previous page*

Geologists (scientists who study Earth) once thought the Grand Canyon was about 6 million years old because that is the age of the Colorado River. In 2008, however, some scientists wrote a paper that led many experts to think the canyon could be much older.

Some geologists today believe the Grand Canyon is closer to 17 million years old than 6 million years old. They point out that just because the Colorado River is 6 million years old does not mean that other flowing water could not have carved some of the Grand Canyon. These geologists think that a river that came before the Colorado River actually carved out much of the canyon. They believe this river flowed in the opposite direction of the Colorado River—north instead of southwest.

No matter how old the canyon is, however, it was created by **erosion.** Water constantly flowing over the land of the Colorado **Plateau** carved, over time, a deep chasm. This chasm was enlarged by the the action of small bits of sand carried by the wind and water, which also wore away at the sides of the cliffs.

Over millions of years, rivers meandering across the high Colorado Plateau (right) cut deep through the rock as the water flowed towards the lowest ground, carving out the Grand Canyon.

At Horseshoe Bend (above),
not far from the entrance to
Grand Canyon National Park,
the Colorado River cuts a sharp
bend through the layers of
sandstone beneath.

The Mariana Trench

Where Is the Mariana Trench and What's Special About It?

The Mariana Trench is a *crescent-shaped* (curved) chasm at the bottom of the western Pacific Ocean. At the Challenger **Deep,** it is 35,840 feet (10,924 meters) from the surface of the ocean to the bottom of the Mariana Trench. That makes it the deepest place in the ocean and the deepest place on Earth. If you put Mount Everest, the highest peak on Earth, at the bottom of the Mariana Trench, there would still be 6,805 feet (2,074 meters) of water above Everest's peak.

The Mariana Trench is about 1,580 miles (2,550 kilometers) long, more than 5 times as long as the Grand Canyon. The trench is, on average, about 43 miles (69 kilometers) wide. The Grand Canyon, however, has been formed by **erosion.** The Mariana Trench was formed in a completely different way, by **plate tectonics.**

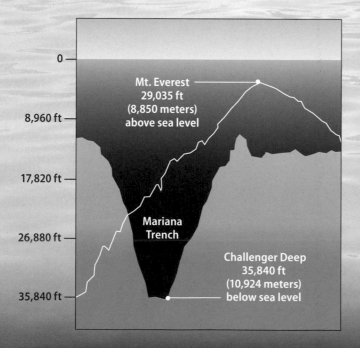

0

Mt. Everest
29,035 ft
(8,850 meters)
above sea level

8,960 ft

17,820 ft

Mariana
Trench

26,880 ft

Challenger Deep
35,840 ft
(10,924 meters)
below sea level

35,840 ft

The Mariana Trench is deeper than Mt. Everest is tall. If you were to place Mt. Everest, the highest mountain on Earth, at the bottom of the Mariana Trench, it would be covered by more than 6,805 feet (2,074 meters) of ocean!

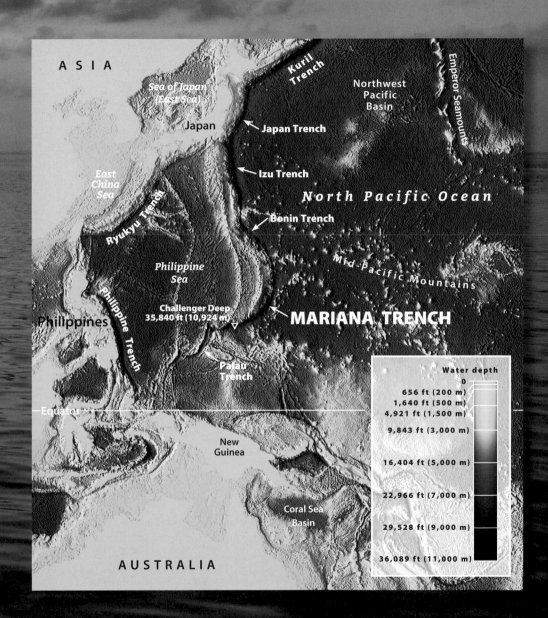

ASIA

Sea of Japan
(East Sea)

Japan

East
China
Sea

Kuril Trench

Northwest
Pacific
Basin

Emperor Seamounts

Japan Trench

Izu Trench

North Pacific Ocean

Bonin Trench

Ryukyu Trench

*Philippine
Sea*

Mid-Pacific Mountains

Philippine Trench

Challenger Deep
35,840 ft (10,924 m)

MARIANA TRENCH

Philippines

Palau
Trench

Equator

New
Guinea

Coral Sea
Basin

AUSTRALIA

Water depth
0
656 ft (200 m)
1,640 ft (500 m)
4,921 ft (1,500 m)
9,843 ft (3,000 m)
16,404 ft (5,000 m)
22,966 ft (7,000 m)
29,528 ft (9,000 m)
36,089 ft (11,000 m)

*The Mariana Trench is a huge,
crescent-shaped chasm in the
Pacific Ocean. It is the deepest of
several trenches in the ocean in
this region of the world. In fact, it
is the deepest place on Earth.*

What Is Life Like in the Mariana Trench?

The trench is darker than anything you can imagine. No light reaches so far down in the ocean. Even at 500 feet (150 meters) below the ocean's surface, there is little if any light. And the deepest part of the Mariana Trench is more than 70 times as deep. This means that animals that live in the trench must feel movements, for example, instead of using vision to find things in such darkness. Most are white or pale since colors cannot be seen.

Also, the water in much of the Mariana Trench is very cold. This far down, the temperature is just a little above freezing. Animals at this depth have to conserve energy to survive in the frigid waters with little food. They are often slow and plodding in their movements—except when food is near. They also grow slowly and may live for more than 100 years. As if this weren't enough, the region is home to several *hydrothermal vents* where temperatures can exceed 200 °F (100 °C). Animals that make their home around these vents thrive in the narrow stretch of sea floor between water too hot and water too cold.

Animals large and small live around the Mariana Trench. These include the shrimplike, giant amphipod (below left) and tiny single-celled foraminifera (below).

22

None of this would really matter to you, though, because you would not be able to survive the **pressure** in the Mariana Trench. Standing on land at about sea level, the pressure of the atmosphere (the gases, such as air, surrounding Earth) pressing upon you is 14.7 pounds per square inch (1.03 kilograms per square centimeter). At the deepest part of the Mariana Trench, known as the Challenger **Deep,** the pressure of the water is more than 8 tons per square inch (1 metric ton per square centimeter). You would be crushed in an instant! It is hard to imagine pressure this great.

The different animals found in the Mariana Trench are highly **adapted** to life under a lot of pressure.

Huge colonies of tubeworms (above left) live close to searing hot hydrothermal vents near the Mariana Trench, while a pale rattail fish (above) swims slowly to conserve energy in the dark, frigid water.

Ships and Explorers of the Deep Sea

Some vessels that explore the ocean at great depths are called bathyscaphes (*bath uh skahfz*), which means *deep ships*. A bathyscaphe usually has two parts to it—a cabin to hold observers and a grouping of tanks called a float. Traditionally, the cabin had thick walls to withstand the **pressure** of the deep sea. Some of the tanks in the float are filled with a substance lighter than water, such as gasoline. Though gasoline is lighter than water, it can resist the crushing pressure of the water at great depths. The float also holds containers full of tons of heavy pellets. To *descend* (lower down), the captain has large empty tanks in the float fill with seawater. Without the buoyancy of the air in the tanks, the heavy craft descends. Bathyscaphes cannot store this air and use it to ascend, as submarines do. The immense pressures of the deep sea would cause any such large tank of compressed air to rupture. When the vessel needs to rise, the captain instead *jettisons* (gets rid of) the pellets and leaves them on the ocean floor. This again makes the craft less dense than the surrounding seawater, and it rises to the surface.

Only twice have people explored the Mariana Trench. In 1960, Swiss ocean scientist Jacques Piccard (1922-2008) and oceanographer Don Walsh (1931-), a lieutenant from the U.S. Navy, spent around 20 minutes on the floor of the Mariana Trench. They visited the trench in the

Jacques Piccard and Don Walsh (close up) onboard the bathyscaphe Trieste. This photo (right) was taken as they prepared for their descent into the Mariana Trench in 1960.

Ships and Explorers of the Deep Sea *continued from previous page*

bathyscaphe *Trieste* (*TREE est, or TREE est eh,* in Italian). The Trieste was named for the city where it was built, on the border between Italy and what is now the nation of Slovenia.

It took around five hours for the *Trieste* to descend to the bottom of the Mariana Trench to a depth of 35,800 feet (10,912 meters). The walls of the **pressure** cabin were 5 inches (12.7 centimeters) thick. When the *Trieste's* searchlights were turned on, Walsh and Piccard saw a fish moving through the cold, dark waters. Only then did scientists know that some sea life could exist at such a depth.

In 2012, Canadian-born filmmaker and explorer James Cameron became the first solo diver to reach the bottom of the trench and explore its depths in an expedition called *DEEPSEA CHALLENGE.* Cameron made his descent in a specially made submarine he helped design called the *DEEPSEA CHALLENGER.* He sat in a small pilot sphere surrounded by steel walls to protect him from the deep ocean pressure, like in the Trieste, but much of the sub was built with a special foam material inside its walls. This foam had millions of tiny air pockets which gave it great strength. Cameron discovered many different kinds of creatures during the expedition, including 68 that had never been documented.

The DEEPSEA CHALLENGER (above) during testing in Australian waters before its voyage

Sinking p
trenches.
the neighl
tense heat

• Diverge
cur where
each othei
crust is cr
below the

• Transfor
tonic plate
Earthqual
action of p

Plate tecto
destructio
boundarie
gent plate
is melted c

Type of Margin		
Motion		
Effect		
Boundary		
Volcanic activit		

The Trieste *(above)*

Auguste (above, left) and Jacques Piccard

James Cameron (above)

EXPLORERS

Jacques Piccard was part of a famous family of explorers. The first bathyscaphe was designed by Jacques Piccard's father Auguste (1884-1962). It was tested in 1948. Auguste and his twin brother Jean also conducted high-altitude research in balloons. In 1953, Auguste and Jacques descended 10,300 feet (3,140 meters) into the Mediterranean Sea in a bathyscaphe named *Trieste*. Jacques used the same vessel to explore the Mariana Trench with Don Walsh.

James Cameron (1954-) has made many famous movies, including *Aliens* (1986), *Avatar* (2009), and *The Terminator* (1984). Cameron became interested in the deep sea because of several movies he has made, including *The Abyss* (1989) and *Titanic* (1997).

The N
tecto

Earth
the **m**
Earth
piece
a bit l
are m
mant
called

The p
The ro
the **as**
asthe
inside
(1300
rock l
centir

The M
where
meets
of bou

• Conv
are wh
Maria

At suc
pushir
plate.
DUHK

The Great Rift Valley

What Animals Live in the Great Rift Valley?

The Great Rift Valley contains some of the oldest, largest, and deepest lakes in the world. It is no surprise that many freshwater fish, reptiles, and **amphibians** make the Great Rift Valley their home.

The Great Rift Valley contains a number of lakes with a very high level of soda or salt. Lake Natron in Tanzania, in East Africa, for example, has both soda and salt. The water in such a lake is **caustic** (*KAWS tihk*). That means it burns or eats away things that come in contact with it. Only animals and plants that are **adapted** for life in such water can survive. Some birds, including some species (kinds) of flamingos, can live in these waters.

Many wonderful mammals live in this part of the world—antelopes, elephants, giraffes, gorillas, hippopotamuses, such big cats as leopards and lions, rhinoceroses, and zebras. It is an amazing place for large and interesting animals. Many of these animals are now threatened, however. Their *habitats* (places they live) are being destroyed by people who want to mine or farm this land. Many of these East African mammals are dying off. Illegal hunting has also reduced the numbers of these animals.

There is another wonderful thing about the area of the Great Rift Valley. It was probably humankind's first home. Most scientists believe that early humans **evolved** in east Africa. The oldest **fossil** that can be definitely called human is about 200,000 years old and comes from the Great Rift Valley. Humans began to *migrate* (move) out of Africa to other parts of the globe perhaps 100,000 years ago.

Lake Nakuru, in Kenya, is a soda lake. The flamingos that live along its shores have adapted to life by the lake. They feed on tiny microorganisms that are adapted to live in the caustic water.

The animals of the Great Rift Valley region: a gorilla mother and her young in Uganda (left) and elephants in Kenya (left below).

35

How Was the Great Rift Valley Formed?

On pages 28 and 29 of this book, you learned about **plate tectonics.** The Mariana Trench has formed where two tectonic plates are moving towards each other—a convergent boundary. The Great Rift Valley is formed at a divergent boundary—a boundary where tectonic plates move away from each other. We know that tectonic plates move slowly. It takes millions of years for the movement of these plates to shape landforms. The Great Rift Valley began forming around 25 million years ago.

Within the Great Rift Valley, three tectonic plates—the African Plate, the Arabian Plate, and the Indian Plate—are all pulling apart. In the East African Rift, the African Plate itself is breaking apart into several pieces. As the tectonic plates pull apart from each other, or as plates break apart, huge openings are created. New **magma** oozes up and hardens in the openings to form new **crust.**

In some areas, oozing magma pushed up the surface, creating vast highlands that surround the valley from Ethiopia in the north to Mozambique in the south. Deep, bowl-shaped *depressions,* or low areas, form in areas where plates move apart to form a wide valley. Some of these depressions became narrow lakes and seas. The Dead Sea and the Red Sea both formed in deep depressions of the Great Rift Valley.